SUNSET ELEMENTARY
MEDIA CENTER

P9-CSU-964

SUNSET ELEMENTARY
MEDIA CENTER

# TOGETHER

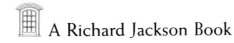 A Richard Jackson Book

26292

SUNSET ELEMENTARY
MEDIA CENTER

# TOGETHER

by George Ella Lyon

pictures by Vera Rosenberry

ORCHARD BOOKS  NEW YORK

A division of Franklin Watts, Inc.

Text copyright © 1989 by George Ella Lyon
Illustrations copyright © 1989 by Vera Rosenberry
All rights reserved. No part of this book may be reproduced or transmitted in any form or by any means,
electronic or mechanical, including photocopying, recording or by any information storage or retrieval
system, without permission in writing from the Publisher.

Orchard Books, a division of Franklin Watts, Inc.
387 Park Avenue South, New York, NY 10016

Orchard Books Canada, 20 Torbay Road,
Markham, Ontario 23P 1G6

Manufactured in the United States of America. Book design by Mina Greenstein
The text of this book is set in 33 pt. Weiss Roman
The illustrations are watercolor and ink line, done by brush, and reproduced in full color.
1   3   5   7   9   10   8   6   4   2

Library of Congress Cataloging-in-Publication Data
Lyon, George Ella, 1949–   Together / by George Ella Lyon ; pictures by Vera Rosenberry. —
1st American ed.   p.   cm.
Summary: An illustrated poem about friendship and togetherness.
ISBN 0-531-05831-X.   ISBN 0-531-08431-0 (lib. bdg.)
1. Children's poetry, American.   [1. Friendship—Poetry.   2. American poetry.]   I. Rosenberry, Vera,
ill.   II. Title.   PS3562.Y4454T64   1989   811'.54—dc19   89-2892   CIP   AC

For Ben
who gave me the refrain
for Joey
newest joy
for Steve
and seventeen years
together

G.E.L.


For Tanya and Julie

V.R.

You cut the timber
and I'll build the house.

You bring the cheese
        and I'll fetch the mouse.

You salt the ice
  and I'll crank the cream.

Let's put our heads together

and dream the same dream.

I'll drive the truck
     if you'll fight the fire.

I'll plunk the keys
    if you'll be the choir.

I'll find the ball
if you'll call the team.

Let's put our heads together

and dream the same dream.

You dig for water
and I'll make a pail.

I'll paint the boat
    if you'll set the sail.

You catch the fish
and I'll catch the stream!

Let's put our heads together

and dream the same dream.

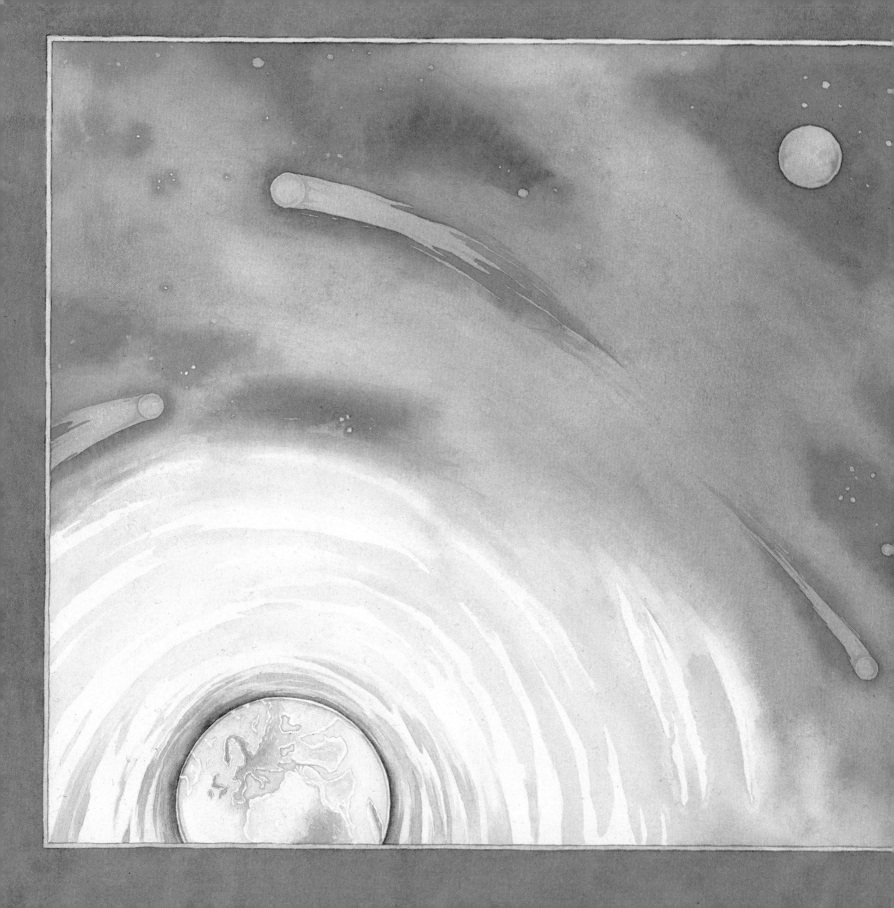

SUNSET ELEMENTARY
MEDIA CENTER

SUNSET ELEMENTARY SCHOOL

811 LYO

TOGETHER

26292